# DOROTHY MEETS ALICE

### or

### The Wizard of Wonderland

**Book and Lyrics
by
Joseph Robinette**

**Music
by
Karl Jurman**

**The Dramatic Publishing Company**
Woodstock, Illinois • London, England • Melbourne, Australia

## *** NOTICE ***

The amateur and stock acting rights to this work are controlled exclusively by THE DRAMATIC PUBLISHING COMPANY without whose permission in writing no performance of it may be given. Royalty fees are given in our current catalogue and are subject to change without notice. Royalty must be paid every time a play is performed whether or not it is presented for profit and whether or not admission is charged. A play is performed anytime it is acted before an audience. All inquiries concerning amateur and stock rights should be addressed to: THE DRAMATIC PUBLISHING COMPANY, 311 Washington St., Woodstock, Illinois 60098.

### COPYRIGHT LAW GIVES THE AUTHOR OR HIS AGENT THE EXCLUSIVE RIGHT TO MAKE COPIES.

This law provides authors with a fair return for their creative efforts. Authors earn their living from the royalties they receive from book sales and from the performance of their work. Conscientious observance of copyright law is not only ethical, it encourages authors to continue their creative work. This work is fully protected by copyright. No alterations, deletions or substitutions may be made in the work without the prior written consent of the publisher. No part of this work may be reproduced or transmitted in any form or by any means, electronic or mechanical, including photocopy, recording, videotape, film, or any information storage and retrieval system, without permission in writing from the publisher. It may not be performed either by professionals or amateurs without payment of royalty. All rights, including but not limited to the professional, motion picture, radio, television, videotape, foreign language, tabloid, recitation, lecturing, publication, and reading are reserved. On all programs this notice should appear: "Produced by special arrangement with THE DRAMATIC PUBLISHING COMPANY of Woodstock, Illinois."

©MCMXC
Book and Lyrics by
JOSEPH ROBINETTE
Music by
KARL JURMAN
Printed in the United States of America
*All Rights Reserved*
(DOROTHY MEETS ALICE or The Wizard of Wonderland)

ISBN 0-87129-079-0

# DOROTHY MEETS ALICE
## or
# The Wizard Of Wonderland

A Musical for Eleven Actors
(Flexible Casting*)
8 women and 3 men—7 men and 4 women

### CHARACTERS

DOROTHY
ALICE
JUDSON
MAD HATTER
SCARECROW
WHITE RABBIT
TIN MAN
DORMOUSE
COWARDLY LION
WICKED WITCH
RED QUEEN

*All animals, as well as the Scarecrow, Tin Man and Mad Hatter, may be played by males or females or any combination thereof.

THE PLACE: The Tulgey Wood.
(Between Oz and Wonderland)

THE TIME: The Present...and the Past.

*DOROTHY MEETS ALICE* was first presented by the Glassboro Summer Children's Theatre with the following cast:

DOROTHY ...................... LEA ANTOLINI
ALICE ........................ LAURA DIAMOND
JUDSON ...................... JAMES BOHANEK
MAD HATTER ............... A. WADE HANCOCK
SCARECROW .................... PATRIC PINTO
WHITE RABBIT .......... DONIELLE LAVANCHER
TIN MAN ...................... MARK JACOBS
DORMOUSE ..................... JOSE ROSARIO
COWARDLY LION .......... BILL WINEGARDNER
WICKED WITCH ............... GWEN HASHEIAN
RED QUEEN .................... KIRSTIN LYNCH

| | |
|---|---|
| Musical Direction by | Rosalind Metcalf |
| Set and lighting by | Bart Healy |
| Costumes by | Joan Sommers |
| Co-produced by | William C. Morris |

# DOROTHY MEETS ALICE

## or

## The Wizard of Wonderland

SETTING: *A clearing in a wooded area. A large bush or clump of trees is upstage. Nailed to an up-center tree is a large rustic sign reading TULGEY WOOD. A similar sign reading OZ, with an arrow pointing off right, and one reading WONDERLAND, with an arrow pointing off left, are also attached to the tree.*

AT RISE: *As the curtain opens, JUDSON WATSON, a teen-age boy, is discovered onstage in a pool of light. The surrounding wooded area is dim. JUDSON looks about in awe and surprise as dreamlike music is heard. He then hears offstage voices. [Note: a sound-effects tape with these voices and other effects is available.]*

DOROTHY'S VOICE *(offstage)*. Toto! Toto!
ALICE'S VOICE *(offstage)*. White Rabbit! White Rabbit!
WHITE RABBIT'S VOICE *(offstage)*. Must hurry! Must hurry! *(The VOICES repeat themselves in unison, followed by laughter from the offstage voices of the WITCH and the QUEEN. A moment later a dog is heard barking offstage. The pool of light on JUDSON fades as the general lights come up.)*

*(DOROTHY, a girl, enters hurriedly.)*

DOROTHY. Toto! Toto! Come back, Toto! *(She exits without seeing JUDSON.)*

*(A moment later, the WHITE RABBIT enters quickly looking at his pocket watch.)*

WHITE RABBIT. Must hurry! Must hurry!

*(He exits as ALICE, a girl, enters.)*

ALICE. White Rabbit! White Rabbit! Where are you, White Rabbit? *(She exits without seeing JUDSON.)*

JUDSON. Hey, wait a minute! Come back! Who are they? What are *they* doing here?...What am *I* doing here? I've never been here before in my life...Maybe I shouldn't be here at all. I might get in trouble...But I'll be in even bigger trouble when I get back home. I haven't done my homework for tomorrow...Book report...My book report!

### (SONG: "OPENING")

JUDSON *(singing).*
> I PUT OFF MY BOOK REPORT 'TIL THE
>     VERY LAST DAY—
> THEN RIGHT AFTER SCHOOL I STARTED
>     TO PLAY
> HOCKEY, MY FAVORITE SPORT.
> I FORGOT ALL ABOUT THE REPORT.
> AFTER DINNER I HEARD MOTHER SAY,
> "OKAY, NO TV 'TIL YOU DO YOUR
>     HOMEWORK!

BETTER START RIGHT AWAY!"
MY LITTLE SISTER STARTED TO SMIRK.
WHEN I CALLED HER A JERK
I WAS SENT OFF TO BED BEFORE I COULD
    LOOK AT A BOOK,
EVEN ONE THAT IS SHORT,
FOR THIS STUPID REPORT
THAT IS DUE TO MY HORROR
TOMORROW!

*(Speaking.)*

Then I made an awesome decision.

I'd get my report from television!

*(Singing.)*

WHAT I MEAN IS, I'D SIMPLY TURN ON
    THE VCR
AND THERE WE ARE—
I'D WATCH IT ON TAPE
AND THAT WOULD BE MY ESCAPE.
I'D LOOK AT A MOVIE INSTEAD,
THEN RUN BACK TO BED,
AND I'D WRITE A REPORT,
KEEPING IT SHORT,
AND FIN'LLY BE THROUGH WITH A
    CHORE
THAT'S A BORE!

SO, WHEN EVERYONE WAS ASLEEP
DOWN THE STAIRS I STARTED TO CREEP.

*(Speaking.)*

I flipped through the tapes as fast as could be,
Looking for a perfect one for me.
"Animal House," and "Mighty Mouse,"
"Stand By Me" and "Rocky III."

*(Other movie titles may be substituted.)*
    Not one did I miss,
    But not a one was on Mrs. Dieffenbaker's approved
    reading list.

*(DOROTHY enters.)*

DOROTHY. Toto! Toto! *(She sees JUDSON for the first time.)* Have you seen my little dog?
JUDSON. Not recently. I mean—no. I'm sorry.
DOROTHY. Oh, dear. Where could he have gotten to? *(She exits. JUDSON starts to follow her, then stops when he hears a dog barking on the other side. He tries to stop DOROTHY, but he is too late.)*
JUDSON. Excuse me. Miss!...Now where was I? Oh, yes—*(Singing.)*
    I STARTED TO GET NERVOUS INSIDE.
    FIN'LLY BEHIND THE TV I SPIED
    AN OLD TAPE THAT I THOUGHT I MISSED.
    WAS IT ON MY READING LIST?
    YES, BEFORE MY EYES IT SUDDENLY
        WAS—/TO MY GREAT SURPRISE—/
    THE WIZARD OF OZ! YEAH!

    I PUT IN THE TAPE, AND BOY WAS I GLAD.
    THIS WAS THE BEST IDEA I'D EVER HAD.
    BUT BEFORE VERY LONG
    I KNEW SOMETHING WAS WRONG.
    I SAW SOMEONE STANDING ON THE
        LANDING.
    THERE IN HIS ROBE STOOD DEAR OLD
        DAD!

*(Speaking.)*
    Boy was he mad.
    I said goodbye to Dorothy and Toto
    As off to bed I had to go.

*(The WHITE RABBIT enters muttering, "Must hurry, Must hurry," then exits. ALICE enters. She sees JUD-SON.)*

ALICE. Excuse me. Have you seen a white rabbit come along this way?

JUDSON. Was he wearing a pocket watch and a waist-coat?

ALICE. Yes.

JUDSON. I—I think he went that way.

ALICE. Thank you ever so much. *(Calling offstage.)* White Rabbit! White Rabbit! *(She exits.)*

JUDSON. But—but—*(He shrugs and sings.)*
    **SO I DUCKED INSIDE MY SISTER'S ROOM,**
    **LIKE INDIANA JONES AND THE TEMPLE**
        **OF DOOM.**
    **I GRABBED THE FIRST BOOK I COULD**
        **FIND**
    **AND LEFT THE EVIL TEMPLE BEHIND.**
    **I GOT TO MY ROOM AND LOOKED AT MY**
        **LIST**
    **THEN SUDDENLY RAISED A VICTORY FIST.**
    **MUCH TO MY RELIEF I HELD IN MY HAND**
    **THE APPROVED ADVENTURES OF ALICE**
        **IN WONDERLAND!**

    **SO INTO MY BED AND UNDER THE**
        **COVERS I TOOK**

PENCILS, PAPER, FLASHLIGHT AND BOOK.
AND I STARTED TO READ
WITH A WHOLE LOT OF SPEED,
BUT BEFORE VERY LONG
I STARTED TO YAWN,
AND I TRIED HARD TO KEEP
FROM FALLING FAST ASLEEP.
I THOUGHT I WAS AWAKE.

*(DOROTHY enters.)*

DOROTHY. Toto! Toto! *(She exits.)*

*(The WHITE RABBIT enters, then exits, ALICE enters.)*

ALICE. White Rabbit! White Rabbit! *(She exits.)*
JUDSON. Toto? White Rabbit?...Dorothy? Alice? And
   me—Judson Watson. All in the same place—at the very
   same time. *(A pause.)* Maybe I'm hibernating. I mean
   hallucinating. And if I *am* hallucinating, how did it hap-
   pen?...Wait a minute. I think I—*(Singing.)*
      —FIGURED IT OUT,
      I THINK I KNOW.
      GOT SO TIRED THAT
      I FELL FAST ASLEEP, FLAT ON MY FACE,
      THAT'S HOW I GOT TO THIS STRANGE
         PLACE.
      SO WHERE AM I NOW?
      I WANNA KNOW HOW CAN THIS
         POSSIBLY BE—
      THIS THING THAT HAS HAPPENED TO ME?
      THE ANSWER IS CLEAR IT WOULD SEEM.
      THIS MUST BE A WONDROUS DREAM!

*(DOROTHY and ALICE enter.)*

DOROTHY. It's no use. I'll never find him.

ALICE. It's no use. I'll never catch him.

BOTH. No use at all. *(They become aware of each other.)*

ALICE. Who—who are you?

DOROTHY. My name is Dorothy. I'm from Kansas.

ALICE. My name is Alice. I'm from London. *(They become aware of JUDSON.)*

JUDSON. My name's Judson. I'm from New Jersey... Weehawken, New Jersey. [Note: Any town or city and state may be substituted.]

DOROTHY. Never heard of it. *(ALICE shakes her head.)*

JUDSON. Weehawken?

BOTH GIRLS. New Jersey.

JUDSON. Well, that's okay. Anyway, I've heard of you.

DOROTHY. You have?

ALICE. Where?

JUDSON. I saw Dorothy on TV.

DOROTHY. TV?

JUDSON. Television. Oh, maybe you were born before television was invented. Anyway, I didn't get to see much. Just the tornado and then when you landed in Oz and met the Munchkins.

DOROTHY. That's right. And Glinda the good witch gave me these ruby red slippers to protect me from harm.

JUDSON. Yes. I saw that, too.

DOROTHY. She also told me I could get back to Kansas by following the Yellow Brick Road to Emerald City—

JUDSON. —to where the Wizard of Oz lives.

DOROTHY. Yes! Will I find him?

JUDSON. I don't know. My dad made me turn off the TV.

ALICE. What about me? How did you hear of me?

JUDSON. In a book. It tells all about how you were chasing a White Rabbit and fell down a rabbit hole into Wonderland.

ALICE. That's right. I did. And I found this little bottle which says "drink me." *(She takes the bottle from her pocket.)*

JUDSON. And if you drink it, you'll become so small—

ALICE. —that hardly anyone can see me.

JUDSON. Right.

ALICE. So what else did the book say? What happens next?

JUDSON. I don't know. I went to sleep.

ALICE. Was I that boring to you?

JUDSON. No, no. It's...it's a long story. *My* story, I mean.

ALICE. Oh, are you also in a book?

DOROTHY. Or on tele—vision?

JUDSON. No, I'm just a kid from Weehawken. But I don't think I'm in New Jersey anymore. My story is just that—I was supposed to write a book report and come to school in the costume of my favorite character. The best costume wins a blue ribbon.

ALICE. But you didn't read the book.

DOROTHY. Or come up with a costume.

ALICE. Because you waited till the very last minute to do your homework.

DOROTHY. Then you fell asleep.

ALICE. And now you're in the middle of a dream.

JUDSON. Well, I'm not the only one. You're both in a dream, too.

ALICE. Don't be silly. I'm in Wonderland.

DOROTHY. And I'm in Oz.

JUDSON. Alice, you fell asleep on the riverbank when your sister was reading to you. That's in the book. Dorothy, you got knocked unconscious during the tornado. That's in the movie.

ALICE. Then I have to get back home as quickly as possible. My sister will be very worried.

DOROTHY. And my Aunt Em and Uncle Henry will be worried, too.

ALICE. I must find the White Rabbit so he can lead me back to the rabbit hole.

DOROTHY. And I must find the Wizard so he can show me how to get back home. But first I have to find Toto. Goodbye, Alice. It was awfully nice to meet you.

ALICE. The pleasure was mine, I'm sure, Dorothy. Good luck.

DOROTHY. Thanks. Bye, Judson.

ALICE. Good luck to you as well.

JUDSON. But wait. If you leave, I'll wake up. And it'll be time for school. And...and—

ALICE. No book report.

DOROTHY. No costume.

BOTH GIRLS. *And* no blue ribbon.

JUDSON *(dejected)*. Yeah. When I get back home I'm gonna be in big trouble. *(Brightening.)* Unless.

ALICE. Unless?

JUDSON. Unless I stay here.

DOROTHY. Here? Forever?

JUDSON. Sure. What's wrong with that?

ALICE. But you'll miss your home—

DOROTHY. Your friends—

BOTH GIRLS. Your family.

JUDSON. Aww. My mom's always making me do my homework. My dad's always making me turn off the TV. And my sister's always making me mad at her.

MAD HATTER'S VOICE *(offstage)*. Mad Hatter? Who called the Mad Hatter?

DOROTHY. Who was that?

JUDSON. Probably just the wind.

ALICE. Judson, you can't stay here all your life.

JUDSON. Why not? There are worse places to spend your life than right here in—what does that sign say?—the Tulgey Wood.

ALICE *(looking at the sign)*. The Tulgey Wood...I think I've heard of this place before.

JUDSON. Great spot. Right between Oz and Wonderland. And the best part—no school, no homework and no sister.

DOROTHY. But when it gets dark here in the wood, you might get scared, you know.

SCARECROW'S VOICE *(offstage)*. Scarecrow? Will someone help the scarecrow?

ALICE. Who was that?

JUDSON. Just an echo, probably. Listen. *(Loudly.)* Ec-ho!

SCARECROW'S VOICE *(offstage)*. Scare-crow.

JUDSON. See? Hey, I've got a great idea. Why don't we all stay right here.

DOROTHY. Don't be silly.

ALICE. We couldn't possibly.

JUDSON. But if you leave, I'll wake up—remember?

DOROTHY. But we have to get back home to our families.

ALICE. Our friends.

BOTH GIRLS. Our playmates.

JUDSON *(taking the GIRLS by the hands)*. Wait a minute. Listen—

(SONG: "STAY WITH ME")

JUDSON *(singing)*.

YOU'LL NEVER NEED TO FIND ANOTHER
BUDDY
IF YOU'RE HERE WITH ME.
YOU'LL NEVER BE WITHOUT A CLOSE
COMPANION
IF YOU'RE NEAR TO ME.

YOU'LL NEVER HAVE A JOURNEY
FRAUGHT WITH DANGER
IF YOU WALK WITH ME.
YOU'LL NEVER LACK FOR LIVELY
CONVERSATION
IF YOU TALK WITH ME.

WILL YOU STAY WITH ME,
EVERYDAY WITH ME?
I'LL MAKE YOUR DREAMS COME TRUE.
COME AND PLAY WITH ME, AND I
GUARANTEE
YOU'LL BE OKAY IF YOU STAY WITH ME!

YOU'LL NEVER HAVE A NIGHTMARE
WHEN YOU'RE SLEEPING
IF YOU DREAM WITH ME.
YOU'LL NEVER LOSE ANOTHER GAME OF
SCRABBLE
IF YOU TEAM WITH ME.

YOU'LL NEVER FIND A FRIEND AS FUN AS
ME.

ALICE.

THOUGH YOU SEEM TO LACK HUMILITY,

DOROTHY.

WE ADMIT WE LIKE YOUR COMPANY.

JUDSON.

THEN YOU BOTH AGREE—
YOU WILL STAY WITH ME,
EVERYDAY WITH ME?

GIRLS.

WILL OUR DREAMS COME TRUE?

JUDSON.

COME AND PLAY WITH ME,
AND I GUARANTEE
YOU'LL BE OKAY IF YOU STAY WITH ME.

((Speaking.)

Okay...I've told you what I'll do for you. Now it's your turn. (The GIRLS huddle for a moment.)

ALICE (singing, to JUDSON).

YOU'LL NEVER GO TO BED WITHOUT
YOUR SUPPER
IF YOU DINE WITH ME.

DOROTHY (to JUDSON).

YOU'LL NEVER FIND YOURSELF IN
STORMY WEATHER
IF YOU SHINE WITH ME.

ALICE.

YOU'LL NEVER MISS A NOTE OR LOSE
THE RHYTHM
IF YOU SING WITH ME.

DOROTHY.

YOU'LL NEVER BE WITHOUT A DANCING
PARTNER
IF YOU SWING WITH ME.

JUDSON and DOROTHY.
> I WILL STAY WITH YOU.

ALICE.
> EVERYDAY—

ALL.
> WITH YOU—
> ALL THE WHOLE WAY THROUGH.

JUDSON.
> I WILL BE YOUR FRIEND
> TO THE VERY END.

DOROTHY.
> WE'LL NEVER, EVER LET IT END—

ALICE.
> —SINCE WE'RE A PERFECT BLEND.

ALL.
> THIS IS WHERE ALL OUR DREAMS COME
> TRUE. *(They dance and mime playing games.)*

ALICE.
> IF YOU DREAM AND TEAM AND DINE
> WITH ME—

DOROTHY.
> IF YOU SING AND SWING AND SHINE
> WITH ME—

JUDSON.
> IF YOU WALK AND TALK ALL THE TIME
> WITH ME
> YOU HAVE MY GUARANTEE

> YOU'RE OKAY.

ALICE.
> OKAY—

DOROTHY.
> OKAY—

ALL.

**IF YOU STAY WITH ME...WE THREE!**

JUDSON *(speaking)*. Does this mean you'll stay?

DOROTHY and ALICE. What do you think?

JUDSON. Okay! *(They join hands and skip around.)*

*( The MAD HATTER enters.)*

MAD HATTER. No, no, no, no—no, no, no! *(DOROTHY, ALICE and JUDSON are startled.)*

DOROTHY and ALICE. Oh!

MAD HATTER. No, no, no, no—no, no, no!

JUDSON. Did you say, "No, no, no, no—

DOROTHY. —no, no—

ALICE. —no"?

MAD HATTER. Yes, yes, yes, yes—yes, yes, yes, I did indeed say, "No, no, no, no—no, no, no!"

ALICE. Who are you anyway, sir?

MAD HATTER. The Mad Hatter, of course, and I'm so mad I could tear a tomtit to tatters.

DOROTHY. Goodness.

JUDSON. Who has angered you so, sir?

MAD HATTER. You don't know, sir?

JUDSON. No, sir.

MAD HATTER *(pointing to DOROTHY)*. Her.

ALICE. Why her?

MAD HATTER *(pointing to ALICE)*. And her.

DOROTHY. Why her?

MAD HATTER *(pointing to JUDSON)*. And you, sir.

JUDSON. Why me, sir?

MAD HATTER. You'll see, sir—

ALICE. Excuse me—must you speak in rhyme?

MAD HATTER. All the time. That's my specialty—riddles, reasons and rhymes. I also do jokes for special occasions. I work hard at being a bard. My card. *(He hands a card to JUDSON.)*

JUDSON. Thanks.

MAD HATTER. Next time you're having a party, give me a call. Make it a tea party, and it's free for all.

DOROTHY. Excuse me, sir, but why are you so mad at us?

MAD HATTER. Because you plan to stay here in the Tulgey Wood.

ALICE. Where *have* I heard of this place before?

DOROTHY. Does the Wood belong to you?

MAD HATTER. No more than it belongs to you.

DOROTHY. Then why don't you want us to stay here?

MAD HATTER. You don't know?

DOROTHY. No.

MAD HATTER. I really need some tea. When I'm really mad, I need some tea. Even when I'm not mad, I need some tea. But I'm always mad, so I would always need some tea anyway, wouldn't I? That's a riddle. My special-*tee*.

DOROTHY. Sir, why don't you want us to stay here?

MAD HATTER. Because people are depending on you.

ALICE. *Who* is depending on us?

SCARECROW'S VOICE *(offstage, muffled)*. Help the Scarecrow!

MAD HATTER. Him, for one.

JUDSON. Him? The echo?

MAD HATTER. That's not an echo, you know.

DOROTHY *(looking offstage)*. It—it looks like a scarecrow.

ALICE *(also looking offstage).* His arms seem to be waving. But the wind's not blowing.

DOROTHY. He couldn't possibly be alive, could he? That only happens in stories.

JUDSON *(to himself).* Or dreams. *(To the OTHERS.)* I'll —I'll go see what he wants. *(He exits. An offstage "screech" is heard at the other side.)*

ALICE. Goodness, what was that? *(Another "screech.")*

MAD HATTER. Such persistence. It appears someone else requires your assistance.

DOROTHY *(looking offstage).* It looks like a man made of tin.

ALICE. A tin man? What could he want of us?

MAD HATTER. A little oil, perhaps, to get him going again?

DOROTHY. Where can I find some oil?

MAD HATTER. Why don't you use the oil can right there next to the fellow. *(Another "screech" is heard.)*

DOROTHY. Good idea. *(She exits.)*

ALICE. But if you knew what he needed—and where the oil was—why didn't *you* help him?

MAD HATTER. It's not part of my contract. I do rhymes, reasons, riddles, occasional jokes and tea. That's it for me.

*(The WHITE RABBIT enters.)*

WHITE RABBIT. Oh, dear, oh, dear, oh, dear. I shall be late.

ALICE. White Rabbit! Wait, wait!

WHITE RABBIT. No time, no time. The Duchess is waiting.

ALICE. But I need you to show me the way back—*(The WHITE RABBIT exits as ALICE chases after him but trips over a large bundle of straw, or hay, and falls.)*. Goodness, what was that?

MAD HATTER. A white rabbit, of course.

ALICE. I know that. I wondered what I fell over.

MAD HATTER. You did *not* fall over a white rabbit.

ALICE. I *know* that.

MAD HATTER. But you do not know that *he* needs you, too.

ALICE. Me?

MAD HATTER. You...or the other young lady—or some-one.

ALICE. Why?

MAD HATTER. I do the riddles around here. Remember?

ALICE. "Why" is *not* a riddle.

MAD HATTER. Don't you mean—*what* is not a riddle?

ALICE. You're absolutely mad.

MAD HATTER. As a hatter!

TIN MAN'S VOICE *(offstage)*. Oh, thank you.

*(The TIN MAN enters, followed by DOROTHY who carries an oil can.)*

TIN MAN *(flexing)*. Thank you ever so much, Miss. I would shake hands with you, but I've forgotten how.

MAD HATTER. Have you gotten a little—*rusty*—over the years? *(He laughs.)* That was a joke.

TIN MAN. I thought it was a riddle.

MAD HATTER. Now I'm mad.

*(JUDSON enters carrying a scarecrow—not live, but a stage prop—over his shoulder.)*

JUDSON. Easy there, old fellow. I'll just set you down over here—

*(He trips over the same straw that ALICE fell over. He and the scarecrow fall down behind a large bush and are hidden from view for a moment. The SCARECROW —now live and closely resembling the stage prop— rises from behind the bush.)*

SCARECROW. Oh, thank you, young feller. I'm much obliged for your kindness. *(He helps JUDSON up from behind the bush.)* Howdy, everybody. Have you ever been stuck in one position for years with nothing but a pole up your back to keep you from falling over?
MAD HATTER. Is that a riddle?
SCARECROW. I don't think so.
MAD HATTER. Good, because that's *my* department.

*(The WHITE RABBIT enters hurriedly looking at his pocket watch.)*

WHITE RABBIT. Oh, dear, oh, dear, oh, dear. I shall be so very, very late.
ALICE. Good. Here he is again. White Rabbit! White Rabbit!
WHITE RABBIT. No time! No time! I must find the Duchess. The Duchess is waiting.
ALICE. But, please. If you could just stop. For only a minute. *(The WHITE RABBIT "freezes," staring at his watch. ALL look at him intently.)*
ALICE *(after a moment)*. Are you...all right?
WHITE RABBIT. All right.
ALICE. Okay?

WHITE RABBIT. Okay.

ALICE. What...are you doing?

WHITE RABBIT. Counting. You said one minute. Ten thousand, eleven thousand—

ALICE. But why are you counting? You have a watch.

WHITE RABBIT. My watch does not have a second hand. Sixteen thousand, seventeen thousand—

MAD HATTER *(taking out his watch, then to ALICE).* He can use mine.

ALICE. But yours doesn't have a second hand either. *(Looking closer.)* It doesn't even tell what *time* it is. It only gives the day of the month. This is getting curiouser and curiouser.

MAD HATTER. Is that good grammar?

SCARECROW. Sounded pretty good to me. 'Course anything sounds okay when all you've heard is crows all your life.

TIN MAN. Or the screech of rusty metal. *(He moves and a slight "screech" is heard.)* May I have a little more oil, please?

DOROTHY. Oh, certainly, Tin Man. *(She takes the can and "oils" him.)*

WHITE RABBIT. Thirty-eight thousand, thirty-nine thousand—

JUDSON. Alice, your minute will be up soon.

ALICE. Oh, I forgot. Please White Rabbit, could you show me the way back to the—

*(A loud "roar" is heard offstage as ALL cringe. The LION enters.)*

LION. All right, put 'em up—put 'em up! Put up your dukes! *(He roars again.)*

DOROTHY. Oh, no. A lion!

LION. You bet I'm a lion. And I'm just dyin' to rip ya to shreds. Tear ya asunder. Then roar like thunder. *(He roars as ALL cringe again.)* Then I'll take ya in my paws and open up my mighty jaws and have the whole bunch-o'-ya for my lunch-o'-ya!

*(He roars again and begins to chase them. A moment later he falls over the pile of straw previously fallen over by JUDSON and ALICE. From underneath the straw rises the DORMOUSE, who yawns.)*

DORMOUSE *(in a cockney accent)*. Can't a fella get a wink of sleep around here? *(ALL are surprised. The LION, on his knees, begins to retreat, sobbing.)*

LION. A mouse...a mouse! Please don't hurt me. I didn't mean to wake ya. Honest I didn't. I hope I didn't make ya sore.

DORMOUSE. Aw, forget it, gov'nor. I'm not a sore mouse. I'm a *dor*mouse.

ALICE. A dormouse?

DORMOUSE. 'At's right, duckie. Bet'cha wonder what I'm doing out-of-doors, eh? *(He laughs and nudges the MAD HATTER with his elbow.)* Guess you're not the only bloke around here with the jokes. Right, gov'nor?

MAD HATTER. Now I'm really mad. *(DOROTHY goes to the LION who is still sobbing.)*

DOROTHY. Poor Mr. Lion. You're not mean or bad or vicious after all.

LION. Please don't let it get out. My reputation would be ruined.

WHITE RABBIT. Sixty thousand. *(To ALICE.)* Your time is up. Now I must go. The Duchess is waiting, wherever she may be. *(He starts to leave.)*

ALICE. Wait, wait. Don't leave. There are so many questions. *(The WHITE RABBIT stops but shows his impatience.)* Why must you find the duchess?

DOROTHY. And why have all of you come here?

JUDSON *(to the MAD HATTER)*. And why are you angry that Dorothy and Alice and I want to stay here in the Tulgey Wood?

MAD HATTER. Young man, where are you from?

JUDSON. Weehawken—New Jersey.

MAD HATTER. Never heard of it.

JUDSON. Weehawken?

MAD HATTER. New Jersey.

JUDSON. It's a state.

MAD HATTER. Are you not more likely from the state of ignorance than from the state of New Jersey?

JUDSON. Is that a riddle?

MAD HATTER. It's a fact. *(Pointing to JUDSON, then to DOROTHY and ALICE.)* Because you, you and you want to stay here while everyone is depending on you.

JUDSON. *Who's* depending on us?

MAD HATTER. *Us.*

ALICE. Curiouser and curiouser.

SCARECROW. We've been waiting a long time—

TIN MAN. —for you to come—

DORMOUSE. —or someone like you—

LION. —we're not sure who—

WHITE RABBIT. —to help us find what we need.

JUDSON. What...*do* you need?

SCARECROW. I, for one, need a brain to replace this old straw I've got up here.

WHITE RABBIT. I need to find the duchess, and I don't know where to look.

TIN MAN. I need a heart to replace this empty feeling right here. *(He bangs on his chest with his fist. A hollow sound is heard.)*

LION. It's obvious what I need. *(He sobs.)*

DOROTHY *(putting her arm around him)*. Courage, Lion.

LION. Yeah, dat's what I need.

ALICE. What about you, Mr. Hatter?

MAD HATTER. I need to find my tea party. I haven't had a cup of steaming hot tea in years.

JUDSON. And the Dormouse?

DORMOUSE. A place to lay me head down without blokes tripping over me all the time.

MAD HATTER. He can join my tea party. That'll keep him awake. Every time he starts to doze, I'll pour tea upon his nose.

DOROTHY. How do you know—we're the ones who are supposed to help?

SCARECROW. We don't, for sure.

TIN MAN. But we've been waiting around so long.

WHITE RABBIT. We hop, hop, hop, uh, hope, hope, hope you're the ones. *(ALL agree.)*

ALICE. Judson, do you understand any of this?

JUDSON *(solemnly)*. I...I think I do. Dorothy...Alice... *(He takes their hands.)* I believe you're the ones who have been sent here to help them. If I'd read the books I'd know for sure. But I get the feeling you're the ones they're waiting for. They're your responsibility. And I have to let you go.

DOROTHY. But when we leave—

ALICE. —you'll wake up.

DOROTHY. No book report.

ALICE. No costume.

BOTH. No blue ribbon.

JUDSON. Well, I guess that's *my* responsibility—facing up to Mrs. Dieffenbaker and saying, "Mrs. D, I didn't do my book report because—because I was sick."

DOROTHY. Judson—

JUDSON. Uh—"because the dog ate it"—?

ALICE. Judson—

JUDSON. Uh—"because the library burned down"—?

ALICE and DOROTHY. Judson—

JUDSON. "Because—I have no excuse."

DOROTHY. That's much better.

WHITE RABBIT *(after a moment)*. So, what is your answer, please?

MAD HATTER. Do you stay here in the Tulgey Wood and avoid your responsibilities?

TIN MAN. Or do you help your fellowman?

LION. And fellow beast?

DOROTHY. Wait a minute…What's the rush? Why don't we stay right here—for a little while at least. This is where I lost Toto. Maybe he'll come back to the Tulgey Wood. *(ALICE turns and looks at the "Tulgey Wood" sign.)* Besides, we don't really know what's out there in Oz and Wonderland. At least here it's safe and sound—

ALICE *(pointing to the "Tulgey Wood" sign)*. And dangerous!

ALL. What?

ALICE. Very dangerous.

ALL. What do you mean? What is she talking about? *(Etc.)*

DOROTHY. *Now* I remember hearing of the Tulgey Wood.

ALICE. You do?

DOROTHY. It's the home of the fearsome Jubjub bird.
*(ALL react in fear.)* The Frumious Bandersnatch. *(More*
*reactions.)* But worst of all, a horrid monster—
LION *(trembling)*. More horrid than me?
SCARECROW. What's it called?

### (SONG: "JABBERWOCKY")

ALICE *(singing)*.
> THERE'S A MONSTER CALLED THE
> JABBERWOCK,
> AND HE LIVES RIGHT HERE IN THE
> TULGEY WOOD.
> AT NIGHT WHEN IT'S DARK HE BEGINS
> TO STALK
> ALL THE CHILDREN IN THE
> NEIGHBORHOOD.
> STAY OUT...OF THE TULGEY WOOD!

> NOW THE JABBERWOCK HAS TWO EYES
> OF FLAME,
> AND THE NOISE HE MAKES IS A BURBLIN'
> SOUND.
> HIS FAVORITE GAME IS TO TRY AND
> MAIM
> ALL THE BOYS AND GIRLS IN A SINGLE
> · BOUND!

> STAY OUT—

ALL.
> OF THE TULGEY WOOD.

ALICE.
> JABBERWOCKY, JABBER-JABBERWOCKY,
>> BAD AS HE CAN BE,
> JABBERWOCKY, JABBER-JABBERWOCKY,
>> STAY AWAY FROM ME.

FIRST VOICE *(speaking)*. That means we can't stay here either.

SECOND VOICE. Oh, no. We're not safe anywhere.

ALL *(singing)*
> JABBERWOCKY, JABBER-JABBERWOCKY,

ALICE.
> BAD AS HE CAN BE,

ALL.
> JABBERWOCKY, JABBER-JABBERWOCKY,
>> STAY AWAY FROM ME!

DOROTHY *(speaking)*. Well, I'm not afraid of that jabberwock.
> We'll stand up to him as one.
> If he dares come knockin' at our door,
> What'll we do, Gang?...

ALL. Run! *(Singing.)*
> LOOK OUT!

> JABBERWOCKY, JABBER-JABBERWOCKY,
>> BAD AS HE CAN BE,
> JABBERWOCKY, JABBER-JABBERWOCKY,
>> STAY AWAY FROM ME. *(ALL dance.)*

> STAY OUT OF THE TULGEY WOOD!

> JABBERWOCKY, JABBER-JABBERWOCKY,
>> BAD AS HE CAN BE,

### JABBERWOCKY, JABBER-JABBERWOCKY, STAY AWAY FROM ME.

**STAY OUT!**

FIRST VOICE *(speaking)*. He's a monster.

ALL *(singing)*.

**OF THE TULGEY WOOD...**

SECOND VOICE *(speaking)*. Makes a burblin' sound.

ALL *(singing)*.

**STAY OUT...**

THIRD VOICE *(speaking)*. Comes out at night.

ALL *(singing)*.

**OF THE TULGEY WOOD...**

FOURTH VOICE *(speaking)*. Stalks children.

ALL *(singing)*.

**STAY OUT...**

FIFTH VOICE *(speaking)*. Eyes of flame.

ALL *(singing)*.

**OF THE TULGEY WOOD...**

SIXTH VOICE *(speaking)*. Most unpleasant fellow.

ALL *(singing)*.

**STAY OUT...LOOK OUT!**

DOROTHY *(speaking)*. Alice, where did you hear of this horrible Jabberwock?

ALICE. I read about him in a book. He's the most fearsome beast that ever was.

JUDSON. You say he comes out at night?

ALICE. If I remember correctly.

JUDSON. Well, that gives us a little time. But I think all of you should leave right away.

DOROTHY. But we don't know what to do.

ALICE. Or where to start.

JUDSON (*after a pause*). Dorothy, you're supposed to meet the Wizard. He's going to help you. Maybe you can take some of these people with you, and the Wizard can help them, too.

DOROTHY. Good idea.

JUDSON. Alice, you can take the others. On the way back to the rabbit hole, maybe they'll find what *they're* looking for.

ALICE. Yes, of course.

WHITE RABBIT. But who goes with whom?

MAD HATTER. I've got it. Let's draw straws. (*He pulls a straw from under the hat of the SCARECROW.*)

SCARECROW. Ouch! What are you doing?

MAD HATTER. Drawing a straw.

SCARECROW. Not from me, if you please. Even if I haven't got a brain, I can still feel pain.

JUDSON. We can choose sides later. First, let's all go into Oz and try to find the Yellow Brick Road. Then we'll come back to Wonderland and look for the path to the rabbit hole. After that, we'll decide who goes with Dorothy and who goes with Alice. (*ALL agree to the plan.*) To Oz?

ALL. To Oz! (*They start to leave. A loud offstage "cackling" laughter is heard, followed by a crash.*)

(*The WITCH appears. She brushes herself off as ALL cringe in fear.*)

WITCH. Those stupid Flying Monkeys. You'd think they could work a stupid fly system, wouldn't you. (*Calling back offstage.*) Next time use more counterweights, you dummies. (*Seeing ALL cringing before her.*) Well, my pretties. So you're coming to Oz are you? Well, I'll get you. Just like I got your little dog, little girl.

DOROTHY. You've got Toto?

WITCH. Every bit of him. In *toto* you might say. *(She laughs loudly, then to the MAD HATTER.)* You're not the only jokester around here, buster. I got a million of 'em.

ALICE. Who...who are you?

WITCH. My friends all call me old W-three, but you can address me as the Wicked Witch of the West. *(ALL gasp.)*

DOROTHY. Oh, no.

WITCH. Oh, yes. Whaddja think I was, the Fairy God-mother? Oh, no. I snatched her up long ago.

DOROTHY. What are you going to do with Toto?

WITCH. I don't know just yet. *(Going to the LION.)* May-be I'll fly up into the sky with him and this overgrown fur ball here—tear 'em to pieces—then let it rain cats and dogs. *(A long laugh.)*

LION *(on his knees)*. Oh, don't do dat. I'm afraid of high places.

WITCH. You're afraid of low places, too, you fragile fe-line. But you won't be alone. I'm going to get *all* of you. *(She laughs and begins to stalk them as they re-treat.)*

DOROTHY. You—you can't get me. I'm wearing the ruby-red slippers that Glinda the good witch gave me.

WITCH. But I've still got your dog. And I'll get your other friends, too. *(She laughs menacingly.)*

DOROTHY. Somebody do something. Dormouse, try to scare her.

WITCH. You think I'm afraid of mice? I eat them for lunch.

ALICE. Tin Man. Hit her with your axe.

WITCH. Go ahead, you anemic alloy. I use axes for toothpicks. No, I've got you all, now, my pretties.

JUDSON. Not yet, you don't. You can't do a thing here.

WITCH. Who are you?

JUDSON. Judson Watson from New Jersey. And please—no Jersey jokes.

WITCH. Are you kidding? I'm from Jersey myself. But if there's a joke around here, it's you—if you think you can stop me.

JUDSON. I can't.

WITCH. Ah—ha.

JUDSON. But the boundary can.

WITCH. Boundary…what boundary?

JUDSON. The boundary line between the Tulgey Wood and the Land of Oz. Oz is right over that line, and until we cross it, we're safe from you. *(The WITCH takes a book from her pocket and flips through it.)*

WITCH. I'll just check that out in my "Witch's Handbook of Boundaries, Jurisdictions, Benedictions, Better Diction and Theme Parks in Your Area." Rats. He's right. *(She slams the book shut as ALL cheer.)*

ALL. Yea, Judson. Good work, young fella. *(Etc.)*

WITCH. Pretty smart, kid. You must be from Weehawken. You snipped me this time, but cross that line and you're mine. Flat cold-busted. *(Calling offstage.)* Okay, you monkeys, get on the counterweights. Old W-three's gonna fly again. Goodbye, my pretties. And remember—if I catch you in the Land of Oz, you'll be the little group that was. Hey, you in the funny hat—I also do poetry. What do you think of that? *(She laughs and exits, then from offstage.)* Not so fast on the ropes. Help! *(Her voice now seems to come from above the offstage area.)* Someday we've gotta fix this fly system, you dummies.

ALL. Thanks, Judson. Good work, Judson. *(Etc.)*

JUDSON. Maybe I helped for a little while, but some of you eventually have to go to Oz.

DOROTHY. That's right. The Wizard is waiting.

SCARECROW. But you can go ahead, Dorothy. The ruby slippers will protect you, and you can get your wish.

DOROTHY. But all of you need to get your wishes granted, too. I'd never leave you behind. Besides, I may need your help to get Toto back.

ALICE. What can we do, Judson? The wicked witch will surely be waiting.

JUDSON. I'm not sure. I need to think about this. In the meantime, why don't we all go to Wonderland? We can at least look for the rabbit hole while we're deciding what to do about Oz.

ALL. Good idea. Let's go. *(Etc.)*

JUDSON. To Wonderland?

ALL. To Wonderland! *(They start to leave as a trumpet fanfare is heard. ALL stop.)*

WHITE RABBIT *(nervously)*. What was that?

MAN'S VOICE *(offstage)*. Bow down! Bow down and pay homage to Her Majesty—the Red Queen of Hearts.

ALICE. The Red Queen of Hearts. Who on earth is that?

MAD HATTER. Sounds like a card to me.

*(The QUEEN enters amid another fanfare or a drum-roll.)*

QUEEN. A card? A card, you say? Who are you calling a card?

MAD HATTER. No one, your, uh, Your Largeness, uh, *Largesse.* I just wanted to give you my card. *(He hands her a card.)*

QUEEN. Do you know what I'm going to do with this? The same that I'm going to do with you. *(She rips the card in half.)* Off with your heads! *(ALL gasp.)*

DOROTHY. But why, Your—Your Meanness, uh, Majesty? Why?

QUEEN. Because you didn't bow down. *(ALL hit the ground immediately in deep bows.)* Didn't you hear my henchman?

TIN MAN *(to the LION next to him).* What's a henchman?

LION. I haven't a hunch, man.

ALICE. But Your—Your Hugeness, uh, Highness, we're bowing down now.

QUEEN. Too late! All constituents of my Queendom are required to bow down immediately on the very first fanfare that announces the royal approach of the royal me.

DORMOUSE. I think I'm gettin' a royal pain.

QUEEN. Oh, you'll get much more than that, you rag-tag rodent. *(Calling offstage.)* Henchmen! Ready your axes for the beheadings. *(ALL quiver at her feet.)* On second thought, this is a small group. I think I'll take care of this little job myself. *(Calling offstage.)* Head henchman, hand me my Handy-dandy Head-Hacking Hicky. *(Two arms are seen thrusting a large head-chopping device—similar to those used in magic shows—onto the stage.)* Thank you, Head Henchman. Tell the other henchmen to relax their axes and save their strength for the masses in Mesopotamia. That'll be a mess. *(She takes the head-chopping device to center stage.)* All right, who's first? *(To ALICE.)* Here's a likely candidate.

DOROTHY. Alice, drink from the bottle that will make you small.

QUEEN. A magic potion, eh. Well, for reminding her of it, maybe *you* can be the first.

WHITE RABBIT *(to the SCARECROW next to him).* Scarecrow. Try to scare her.

SCARECROW. I've scared plenty of crows before but never an old hen.

QUEEN. I heard that. *(Standing over the SCARECROW.)* An old hen, am I? Just for that remark, *you're* first, you stupid stack of straw! *(She pulls him up. He runs away yelling "help" and exits.)*

QUEEN *(chasing him, calling offstage).* Henchmen, henchmen, head him off, then off with his head.

DOROTHY. This is terrible. Somebody do something.

MAD HATTER. I've got it. I'll tell her my best joke. When she's doubled over with laughter, we'll push her into that contraption.

ALICE. And cut off her head? *(In disgust.)* Ooo.

MAD HATTER. We won't cut off her head. *(Examining the head-chopping device.)* But it has a lock on it. We'll lock her in till we escape.

DOROTHY. Escape to where? The witch is in Oz. The queen's henchmen are in Wonderland. And the Jabberwock is right here. *(The QUEEN is heard yelling offstage, "Come back, come back.")*

ALICE. Shh! Here they come.

*(The SCARECROW runs on and tries to hide. A moment later, the QUEEN enters hurriedly.)*

ALICE *(whispering to the MAD HATTER)*. Mad Hatter, quickly, your joke.

MAD HATTER *(diverting the QUEEN's attention to himself)*. Oh, yes. Excuse me, Your Highness.

QUEEN. Yes, Your Lowness?

MAD HATTER. Why is a king always short?

QUEEN. Is this a riddle or a joke?

MAD HATTER. I'll let the queen decide, Your Worship.

QUEEN. Very well. Why is a king always short?

MAD HATTER. Because a ruler is only twelve inches long. *(ALL except the QUEEN force laughter.)* Twelve inches long. Get it?

QUEEN. Yes, I got it, and you're going to get it, too. That wasn't a joke *or* a riddle. It was stupid!

MAD HATTER. Royalty's always been a tough audience for me. I hated playing the palace.

QUEEN. You're gonna find out just how tough an audience I really am, you dodo. *You* can be the first victim in my Handy-dandy Head-Hacking Hicky.

MAD HATTER. But I'm sure my head's too big—what with the hat and all.

QUEEN. Don't worry. The Handy-dandy Head-Hacking Hicky is adjustable. One size fits all. *(She laughs and drags him toward center as he protests.)*

DOROTHY *(on her knees, going to JUDSON)*. Judson. Tell her about the boundary. *(She whispers to him.)*

JUDSON. Oh, yeah. Just like we did with the witch. *(The MAD HATTER has been fitted into the head-chopping device. The QUEEN is ready to drop the blade.)* Your—Your Rudeness, uh, Redness.

QUEEN. What is it? Quit stalling.

JUDSON. You can't cut off our heads.

QUEEN. Why not?

JUDSON. Because you're the Queen of Wonderland. Wonderland is over there. *We're* over here. That's your territory. This is ours.

QUEEN *(after a brief pause)*. Let me check that out in my handbook, "The Royal Shaft." *(She takes a book from her pocket.)* "Territories, Promontories, Dormitories, Whigs and Tories and Four-star Restaurants in Your Neighborhood." Rats, he's right. *(ALL cheer as she slams the book shut.)* Who are you anyway?

JUDSON. Judson Watson from Weehawken, New Jersey. But I'm sure you've never heard of it.

QUEEN. Weehawken?

JUDSON. New Jersey.

QUEEN. Sure I have. I used to have a pen pal in Jersey. I wonder what ever happened to the little dear?

MAD HATTER *(pointing to his head)*. Your Surliness, uh, Worthiness. If you don't mind.

QUEEN *(releasing the MAD HATTER from the device)*. Very well, you're spared for now. There'll be no head-hacking today. *(ALL cheer. The QUEEN calls offstage.)* Henchmen! Keep your axes aloft! If one of these simpletons dares set foot in Wonderland, it's off with his head! *(She picks up the head-chopping device and begins to exit to a drumroll and a fanfare. At the end of the long, loud fanfare, ALL including the QUEEN hold their hands over their ears.)* I hate when that happens. *(She exits. ALL breathe a sigh of relief and thank JUDSON.)*

ALICE. That was close. But what shall we do now?

DOROTHY. Alice, at least *you* can escape. All you have to do is drink from the bottle and become small.

ALICE. But then I wouldn't be able to help those who want to go on my adventure with me. *(Turning to JUDSON.)* What shall we do, Judson?

JUDSON. We've got to get out of the Tulgey Wood and away from the Jabberwock—that's for sure. We'll have to escape through Oz—or Wonderland.

DOROTHY. But the witch—

ALICE. And the queen—

JUDSON. We'll just have to take a chance that we won't get caught. We'll divide up. Half of us will search for the Yellow Brick Road. The other half can look for the path to the rabbit hole. We'll go in pairs. While one of you is looking for the passage way, the other can look out for danger. We'll meet back here before sundown. Quickly now. Scarecrow, you and the White Rabbit—to Oz.

WHITE RABBIT. Come along. Must hurry, must hurry.

SCARECROW. Slow down, partner. I'm made outta straw —not grease. *(He and the WHITE RABBIT exit.)*

JUDSON. Dormouse and Tin Man to Wonderland.

TIN MAN. Onward, onward, my sleepy sentinel. Let us show our metal.

DORMOUSE. Take it easy, Gov'nor. It takes a minute to get me tail in gear. *(He and the TIN MAN exit.)*

JUDSON. Mad Hatter—Cowardly Lion. To Oz.

LION. Okay, if he'll keep his jokes to himself.

MAD HATTER. How can I—when I'll be accompanied by a punch-lion? Get it? A punch lion?

LION. I got it. And you're gonna get it, too. *(He chases the MAD HATTER offstage.)*

MAD HATTER *(offstage)*. You're a coward. Don't forget that—a *coward.*

JUDSON. Alice and Dorothy—to Wonderland. And be careful.

ALICE. Hurry, Dorothy.

DOROTHY. I can't move fast in these new slippers. I'll just take them off till we get back. *(She takes off the slippers.)* Come on, Alice. What are you doing?

ALICE *(on her knees)*. Don't rush me. I think I've lost my potion bottle.

DOROTHY. You can find it when we get back. Anyway, you might get that fancy dress all dirty.

ALICE. Don't you mean soiled?

JUDSON. Hurry, you two.

DOROTHY *(as they leave)*. In Kansas, we call it dirt.

ALICE. In London, it's soil. *(They exit.)*

JUDSON. Good. Now *I* can go with—there's nobody else to go with. I know. I'll climb that hill back there and watch out for the witch and queen *and* the Jabberwock who lives right here in the Tulgey Wood. Oh, boy... this dream is suddenly turning into a nightmare. *(He exits.)*

*(The WITCH and QUEEN enter at opposite sides of the stage. They do not see each other. They appear to be searching for something. They begin to walk backward, suddenly bumping into each other.)*

WITCH. Who are you?

QUEEN. Who are *you?*

WITCH. Well, for your information, my pret—I started to say, "my pretty," but that doesn't seem to apply in this case. For your information, I'm a witch.

QUEEN. And for your edification, I'm a queen.

WITCH. I'm a wicked witch.

QUEEN. I'm a mean queen.

WITCH. I'm a wickeder witch than you're a mean queen.

QUEEN. I'm a meaner queen than you're a wicked witch.

WITCH. They don't call me Wilhelmina, the wickedest witch of the west for nothing.

QUEEN. And they don't address me as Quinella, the meanest queen you've ever seen for naught.

WITCH *(in a boxer's stance)*. I'll show you who's the worst.

QUEEN *(taking a karate stance)*. I'll show you who's the worst. *(They start to fight, then pause.)*

WITCH. Wait a minute. Did you say your name was— Quinella?

QUEEN. Indeed. And did you state your name to be— Wilhelmina?

WITCH. Sure did.

QUEEN *(pondering it)*. Wilhelmina.

WITCH *(in thought)*. Quinella. *(A pause.)*

BOTH. My pen pal! *(They embrace.)*

QUEEN. After all these years.

WITCH. That we should finally meet.

QUEEN. It's a small dream, isn't it?

WITCH. So, what are you doing here, my dear?

QUEEN. I'm hoping to get that bottle of shrinking potion from that abysmal Alice. And you?

WITCH. I'm after the ruby red slippers that are on the feet of that detestable Dorothy. *(They search around for a moment.)*

QUEEN. You know...I hate to admit this. But those girls sort of remind me of the way we must have been—in our younger days.

WITCH. It's true. Back when we were pen pals.

(SONG: "WE COULD HAVE BEEN LIKE THEM")

QUEEN.
>WE COULD HAVE BEEN, YOU KNOW, A
>>LOT LIKE THEM,
>QUITE PROPER, PERT AND PRIM,
>NICE AND NEAT,
>GOOD AND SWEET,
>AND CUTENESS TO THE BRIM.

WITCH.
>WE COULD HAVE BEEN A LOT LIKE
>>OTHER GIRLS
>WITH RIBBONS, BOWS AND CURLS,
>FRILLS AND FLUFF,
>ALL THAT STUFF,
>A COUPLA CULTURED PEARLS.

*[Note: Lines designated as BOTH may be assigned individually if desired.]*

·BOTH *(speaking).* Nah! *(Singing.)*
>FOR WE WERE DESTINED TO A CALLING
>>MORE APPALLING,
>APPEALINGLY BIZARRE.

>THE STARS, THE FATES
>GAVE US THE TRAITS
>THAT MADE US WHAT WE ARE.

>WE'RE VILLAINS, WE'RE VILLAINS,
>WE'RE ALWAYS MORE THAN WILLIN'
>TO DO A NASTY LITTLE CHORE
>LIKE GIVE THE WHIP A CRACK,
>TIE A VICTIM TO THE TRACK,
>YOU SEE, WE'RE ROTTEN TO THE CORE.

WE'RE VILLAINS, WE'RE VILLAINS
IT'S ALTOGETHER THRILLIN'
TO FULFILL THOSE NECESSARY NEEDS—
GIVE AN ORPHAN KID A WHACK,
TIE A PUPPY IN A SACK
WE LOVE TO DO THOSE DIRTY DEEDS!

WITCH *(speaking)*. As an ambitious young lady, I was often tempted to go into another line of work. But what other occupation allows you to be such a nasty jerk?

QUEEN. As leader of the Free World, I've often been asked by kings and presidents for my sage advice. I delight in telling them—"Go fry ice."

WITCH *(singing)*.

I COULD HAVE HAD A REGULAR JOB
LIKE ANY COMMON SLOB—
BEAUTY QUEEN,
COLLEGE DEAN,
ACCOUNTANT FOR THE MOB.

QUEEN.

I COULD HAVE BEEN A POTENTATE
WHO HELPED OUT HEADS OF STATE—
NERO AND ROME,
SAVINGS AND LOAN,
AND EVEN WATERGATE.

BOTH *(speaking)*. Nah! *(Singing.)*

FOR WE WERE DESTINED TO A FUTURE
    MORE EXCITING,
MORE FRIGHT'NINGLY BIZARRE.

THE STARS, THE FATES
GAVE US THE TRAITS
THAT MADE US WHAT WE ARE.

WE'RE VILLAINS, WE'RE VILLAINS
WE'RE ALWAYS MORE THAN WILLIN'
TO DO WHAT NORMAL FOLKS ABHOR.
LIKE KICK THE SHERIFF'S SHIN,
SOCK HIS SIDEKICK IN THE CHIN,
BUT WAIT AND SEE, THERE'S PLENTY
    MORE.
WE'RE VILLAINS, WE'RE VILLAINS
IT'S ALTOGETHER THRILLIN'
TO FULFILL THOSE NECESSARY NEEDS—
STICK THE HERO WITH A PIN
STEAL AWAY HIS HEROINE.
WE LOVE TO DO THOSE DIRTY DEEDS!

*(They dance.)*

WITCH *(speaking)*. Do you think a chorus line might need
us?

QUEEN. Will the Rockettes ever heed us?

WITCH. Is June Taylor stalling for us?

QUEEN. Is Busby Berkeley calling for us?

BOTH. Nah! *(Singing.)*

WE'RE VILLAINS, WE'RE VILLAINS,
WE'RE ALWAYS MORE THAN WILLIN'
TO DO AN ODD JOB NOW AND THEN—
LIKE DYNAMITE THE PAYROLL TRAIN,
THEN HIGHJACK THE AIR MAIL PLANE.
WE WORK WITH SKILL AND DISCIPLINE,

WE'RE VILLAINS, WE'RE VILLAINS,
IT'S ALTOGETHER THRILLIN'
TO FULFILL THOSE NECESSARY NEEDS—
STAB A GOOD FRIEND IN THE BACK,
MAKE HIM SIT DOWN ON A TACK.
STEAL SOME CANDY FROM A TYKE,

PUSH A KID RIGHT OFF HIS BIKE.
FILL A SUNNY DAY WITH RAIN,
DRIVE THE AUDIENCE INSANE.
WE LOVE TO DO THOSE DIRTY DEEDS!
*(Speaking.)*
    Hey!

WITCH *(seeing the slippers)*. Ah, the slippers! *(She picks them up.)*

QUEEN *(seeing the bottle)*. Ah, the bottle! *(She picks it up.)*

WITCH. Now, the little pretties no longer have their protection.

QUEEN. So we can get *them* as well as their motley crews.

WITCH. Well, to Oz, so that I can get on with my business.

QUEEN. And on to Wonderland where the beheadings can begin. *(They start to leave.)*

WITCH *(a sudden thought)*. Quinella, my dear.

QUEEN. Yes, Wilhelmina, my sweet.

WITCH. I have an idea. Why don't we work together and wipe out the whole bunch of them at the same time?

QUEEN. I see gears turning between your ears.

WITCH. I have mischief on my mind. Come here. *(She whispers to the QUEEN, pointing to the "Tulgey Wood" sign.)*

QUEEN. Ooo. Devilishly delightful idea. Yes, I think we *can* persuade *him* to do the job.

WITCH. *He'll* do the dirty work even better than us.

QUEEN. You know, Wilhelmina, after this, why don't we go back to being pen pals again?

WITCH. Absolutely, Quinella. But next time, let's be *poison* pen pals.

*(They laugh and exit quickly together. A moment later, JUDSON enters.)*

JUDSON. No sign of the witch *or* the queen—yet. And it's still daylight, so we're safe from the Jabberwock a little longer. I hope everybody's working real hard to find the path to the rabbit hole and the Yellow Brick Road. They should be reporting back soon. I hope they're working together well. Everyone seems to be very friendly with each other.

*(SCARECROW and WHITE RABBIT enter.)*

SCARECROW. It's all your fault.

WHITE RABBIT. No, no, no. The fault is yours.

JUDSON. What's wrong? What happened?

SCARECROW. We can't work together, that's all.

WHITE RABBIT. It is he. Moves much too slowly to suit me.

SCARECROW. And he goes too fast. Always in a big hurry.

WHITE RABBIT. It's the nature of a white rabbit to be in a hurry and get the job done.

SCARECROW. And it's the nature of a scarecrow to be still—and observe what's going on.

JUDSON. But that's okay, don't you see? You can both do your jobs even better working together. While he's being vigilant and looking out for danger, you're racing ahead to the goal.

(SONG: "PERFECT TOGETHER")

JUDSON *(singing)*.
> YOU LIKE TO RUSH, BUT YOU HAVE
> PATIENCE,
> THAT'S NO CAUSE FOR A SPAT!
> YOU'LL FIND A LOT OF COMBINATIONS
> SO MUCH WORSE THAN THAT.

> YOU'RE PERFECT, PERFECT TOGETHER
> LIKE ICE CREAM AND CHOC'LATE CAKE.
> YOU'RE PERFECT TOGETHER,
> WHAT A TEAM YOU MAKE.

*(The SCARECROW and WHITE RABBIT consider the idea for a moment, then shake hands in agreement.)*

*(A moment later, the TIN MAN and DORMOUSE enter.)*

TIN MAN *(speaking)*. I refuse. I refuse!

DORMOUSE. No ya don't, ya squeaky bloke. *I* refuse.

TIN MAN *(to JUDSON)*. He wants to sleep all the time.

DORMOUSE *(to JUDSON)*. To preserve me strength, Gov'nor. Anyway he's so bloomin' active, I can't relax at all.

JUDSON *(singing to DORMOUSE)*.
> YOU LIKE TO REST, WHILE HE STAYS
> BUSY—
> THAT'S NOT A CAUSE FOR ALARM.
> DON'T LET IT GET YOU IN A TIZZY—
> IT WILL CAUSE NO HARM.

WHITE RABBIT *(to DORMOUSE)*
> YOU CAN BE SAVING ENERGY
> WHILE HE'S MAKING HAY UNDER THE
>   SUN.

SCARECROW *(to TIN MAN)*.
> THEN WHEN YOU NEED TO RELAX, YOU
>   SEE,
> HE CAN SHOW YOU HOW IT'S DONE.

JUDSON.
> YOU'RE PERFECT, PERFECT TOGETHER
> LIKE ICED TEA AND APPLE PIE.
> WHATEVER THE WEATHER,
> YOU'LL BE FLYING HIGH.

WHITE RABBIT and SCARECROW.
> YOU'RE PERFECT, PERFECT TOGETHER—
> JUST LOOK INTO A MIRROR, AND YOU
>   WILL SEE—

TIN MAN and DORMOUSE.
> THAT WE'RE PERFECT TOGETHER—
> WE FIT PERFECTLY! *(They shake hands.)*

*(A moment later, the MAD HATTER and LION enter.)*

MAD HATTER *(speaking)*. You still haven't answered my riddle.

LION. I've got a riddle of my own. Why do you talk so much?

MAD HATTER *(to DORMOUSE)*. He's no help at all. Totally lacking in the art of conversation.

LION. I'm used to the woods where it's peaceful and *quiet.*

TIN MAN *(to LION)*. But that's quite all right, you know
   ...*(Singing.)*
   HE LIKES TO TALK, AND YOU LIKE
      SILENCE,
   THAT'S NOT A CAUSE FOR DESPAIR.
DORMOUSE *(to MAD HATTER)*.
   IF YOU WERE STRANDED ON AN ISLAND,
   YOU'D BE GLAD HE'S THERE.
WHITE RABBIT.
   IF YOU'RE NOT ALIKE THAT'S QUITE ALL
      RIGHT.
   OPPOSITES OFTEN ATTRACT.
SCARECROW.
   WHAT WE SEEM TO LACK IN OURSELVES
      IS SLIGHT
   WHEN A FRIEND TAKES UP THE SLACK.
SCARECROW, WHITE RABBIT, DORMOUSE and TIN MAN.
   YOU'RE PERFECT, PERFECT TOGETHER,
JUDSON.
   LIKE BERRIES AND FRESH WHIPPED
      CREAM.
ALL *(except LION and MAD HATTER)*.
   SO NEVER DOUBT WHETHER
   YOU'RE AN IDEAL TEAM.
LION and MAD HATTER *(shaking hands)*.
   WE'RE PERFECT, PERFECT TOGETHER.
   IF WE LOOK INTO A MIRROR, WE WILL
      SEE
   THAT WE'RE PERFECT TOGETHER—
   WE FIT PERFECTLY.
ALL.
   EVERYTHING IS SO MUCH BETTER NOW
   THAT WE'VE BECOME SO ATTACHED.

> IT'S NICE TO SEE THAT WE CAN BE A
> TEAM THAT'S PERFECTLY MATCHED.

JUDSON.

> YOU'RE PERFECT, PERFECT TOGETHER.
> ABOUT THAT THERE'S NO MISTAKE.
> NOW SING ALL TOGETHER—

ALL.

> WHAT A TEAM WE MAKE!

*(DOROTHY enters, followed by ALICE.)*

DOROTHY *(speaking)*. Well, I'm sorry you feel that way.

ALICE. And I regret your attitude, as well.

JUDSON. Oh, no. Not them, too.

DOROTHY *(to JUDSON)*. She made fun of the way we dress back home. Not fancy enough for her, I guess.

ALICE *(to JUDSON)*. Well, she laughed at the way we talk where I come from. Making sport of my accent, I suppose. *(They begin to argue. JUDSON separates them.)*

JUDSON. Now just a minute. Look at it another way...

> *(Singing.)*

> YOU'RE FROM LONDON, YOU FROM
> KANSAS—
> THINK OF ALL THE THINGS YOU CAN
> SHARE.
> LET'S BE GRATEFUL WHEN LUCK HANDS
> YOU
> SOMEONE FROM ELSEWHERE.

ALL *(except DOROTHY and ALICE)*.

> YOU'RE PERFECT, PERFECT TOGETHER,

JUDSON.

> LIKE BROWNIES AND HAWAIIAN PUNCH.

ALL *(except DOROTHY and ALICE)*.

**WHEREVER YOU GATHER,**
**YOU'LL BE QUITE A BUNCH.**
DOROTHY and ALICE *(shaking hands).*
**PERFECT, PERFECT TOGETHER,**
ALL.
**IF WE LOOK INTO A MIRROR WE WILL**
**SEE WE'RE**
**PERFECT TOGETHER—**
WHITE RABBIT, SCARECROW and LION.
**LIKE SUMMER DAYS AND HONEYBEES,**
DORMOUSE, TIN MAN and MAD HATTER.
**ZOO PARADES AND CHIMPANZEES,**
JUDSON, DOROTHY and ALICE.
**OPEN SLEIGHS AND CHRISTMAS TREES!**
DOROTHY AND ALICE.
**WE'RE PERFECT TOGETHER—**
ALL.
**AND THAT'S THE WAY WE'LL ALWAYS BE!**
*(The TIN MAN, LION and SCARECROW join DORO-*
*THY, seemingly arbitrarily, while the WHITE RABBIT,*
*DORMOUSE and MAD HATTER join ALICE.)*
*(Speaking.)*
Perfect!
*(JUDSON glances at the TWO GROUPS.)*
JUDSON. Now I think I know who goes to Oz—and who
goes to Wonderland. *(ALL cheer. A moment later, an*
*offstage "roar" is heard.)*
ALICE. Oh, no.
DOROTHY. What was that?
ALICE. It must be...the Jabberwock.
DOROTHY. But you said he comes out at night.
ALICE. I guess he comes out in the daytime, too. *(An-*
*other "roar.")*

JUDSON. Hurry, you've got to get out of here!

DOROTHY. But what about you, Judson?

ALICE. What will you do?

JUDSON. Don't you remember? When you're gone, I'll wake up. *(A louder "roar.")* I think. *(Another "roar.")* I *hope.*

DOROTHY. Goodbye, Judson.

ALICE. Thank you for every—*(Another "roar.")*

JUDSON. No time for goodbyes. Hurry up, now. You have to get out of here before the witch and the queen know you're leaving. *(DOROTHY and her GROUP start to exit but are stopped by a "cackling" laughter offstage.)*

WITCH'S VOICE *(offstage).* Going somewhere, my pretties?

DOROTHY. Oh, no. *(ALICE and her GROUP start to exit.)*

QUEEN'S VOICE *(offstage).* Well, well, well, my henchmen, look who's *heading* our way. *(She laughs.)*

ALICE. We're too late.

JUDSON. Watch out!

*(The JABBERWOCK enters to loud underscored music. He is a longbodied monster, making a terrible noise. He chases EVERYONE about, knocking most of them to the ground. At last, JUDSON is able to grab the BEAST's head in a "bull-dogging" fashion.)*

JUDSON *(holding the head of the JABBERWOCK as it roars and tries to free itself).* Dorothy, Alice, everybody! Get out of here as fast as you can.

ALICE *(going to her fallen GROUP).* Mad Hatter, White Rabbit, Dormouse! Are you all right?

DOROTHY *(to her GROUP).* Come on, Scarecrow. Get up, Tin Man. Hurry, Lion.

*(Again, the JABBERWOCK roars and struggles with JUDSON who loses his balance. With the head of the JABBERWOCK in his arms, he falls backward, pulling the head and body of the monster away from the two people inside—the WITCH and the QUEEN—who are attired in turn-of-the-century bathing suits which resemble colorful underwear. JUDSON drops the "lifeless" JABBERWOCK to the ground. During the ensuing dialogue he may take the JABBERWOCK offstage, then re-enter quietly.)*

DOROTHY. The witch!

ALICE. The queen!

SCARECROW. It was them all along.

QUEEN *(to WITCH)*. I knew this was a rotten idea, you ninny!

WITCH *(to QUEEN)*. Watch who you're calling a ninny, you numbskull!

QUEEN. A numbskull, am I? Just for that, I'm going to reveal your secret.

WITCH. What secret?

QUEEN. That you didn't capture that little dog after all. He escaped.

DOROTHY. Toto's okay? How wonderful!

WITCH. Just for that, I'm going to tell them *your* secret.

QUEEN. What secret?

WITCH. That you don't really cut off heads after all.

JUDSON. I thought that was kinda weird.

WITCH. That what you really like to do is play croquet with hedgehogs and flamingos.

JUDSON. Now that's *really* weird.

ALICE. Pardon me, but how could you be here in the Jabberwock. We heard your voices over there and over there just before the Jabberwock entered.

QUEEN. My head henchman can imitate my voice perfectly.

WITCH. And my main monkey is a marvelous mimic.

DOROTHY. Excuse me, but if you were *pretending* to be the Jabberwock, where's the *real* Jabberwock?

WITCH. There's no such thing as a Jabberwock.

ALICE. But there is, too. And he lives in the Tulgey Wood. I read about it—in a book.

QUEEN. A book of *poetry*. It's just a poem, silly girl.

ALICE. A poem? Oh yes. That's right. I read the poem when I took a trip through the Looking Glass.

JUDSON. The what?

ALICE. Looking Glass. That was right before my trip down the rabbit hole.

JUDSON. Why don't you just go to Disney World like everybody else?

ALICE. What's Disney World?

DOROTHY. It's probably a lot like Kansas.

WITCH. Well, we didn't get you this time, my pretties.

QUEEN. But we'll get you when you leave the Tulgey Wood. *(Calling offstage.)* Standby, my henchmen. When they come through, whack them with your croquet mallets.

WITCH *(calling offstage)*. Get ready, flying monkeys. If they try to come to Oz, we'll make monkeys out of them.

QUEEN. Well, Wilhelmina, after this fiasco, I'd say you're the biggest monkey of all.

WITCH. Who are you calling a monkey, you big ape? *(She throws the slippers at the QUEEN who dodges them.)*

DOROTHY *(catching the slippers)*. My ruby slippers!

QUEEN. I'm calling *you* a monkey, you baboon. *(She throws the bottle at the WITCH who ducks under it.)*

ALICE *(catching the bottle)*. My potion bottle!

WITCH. How dare you throw things at me. *(Chasing the QUEEN.)*

QUEEN. How dare you throw insults at me. *(She runs from the WITCH.)*

WITCH *(chasing the QUEEN offstage)*. If I looked like you, I'd expect insults, you overripe striped tomato.

QUEEN. At least I don't look like a skinny zebra with a cone on top of my head. *(She exits upstage, followed by the WITCH.)*

WITCH *(offstage)*. Oh yeah? Well, it would only improve your looks, my *ugly*.

QUEEN *(offstage)*. At least my looks *can* be improved, my *homely*. *(They are heard to continue arguing offstage in the distance.)*

JUDSON. Hurry, everybody. While they're still arguing, you can get away.

DOROTHY. Thank you, Judson.

ALICE. You saved our lives, you know.

JUDSON. Well, maybe not your lives...but your stories at least.

DOROTHY. Poor Judson. Soon you'll have to wake up—without your book report.

ALICE. *Or* your costume.

DOROTHY. *Or* a blue ribbon.

JUDSON. I guess that's the story of *my* life. *(ALL except DOROTHY, ALICE and JUDSON huddle in the background.)*

DOROTHY. Maybe Mrs. Dieffenbaker will let you turn in your book report a little late. For partial credit, anyway.

JUDSON. Maybe. Especially if I promise to read my books on time *every* time from here on in.

ALICE. Maybe she'll let you bring your costume in late as well.

JUDSON. No. Everybody's supposed to wear their costumes on the same day. Tomorrow.

MAD HATTER *(as the "huddle" breaks up, pointing to his watch).* Correction. Not tomorrow. *Today.*

JUDSON. Yeah. I guess it's getting close to morning back home. When I wake up, it'll be time for school. I wouldn't have time to make a costume, anyway.

TIN MAN. Unless—

JUDSON. Unless what?

WHITE RABBIT. Unless we help you.

JUDSON. How can you possibly help me with a costume?

SCARECROW. By each of us giving you something of our own.

DORMOUSE. —as a little token of appreciation—

LION. —for all you've done for us. *(Each, in turn, hands JUDSON an item.)*

TIN MAN. My axe for your bravery.

WHITE RABBIT. My waistcoat for your warmth.

SCARECROW. My gloves for your helping hands.

DORMOUSE. Me scarf, Gov'nor, for stickin' your neck out for us.

MAD HATTER. My hat for always using your head.

LION. And my tail. For standing behind us one-hundred-percent. *(He pulls off his tail.)* Ouch. How's dat for courage.

JUDSON *(holding all the "gifts")*. Gosh. Thanks, everybody. I don't know what to say.

LION. Shucks, folks, he's speechless.

DOROTHY. You don't have to say anything, Judson.

ALICE. Just don't forget us.

DOROTHY. And don't forget to read about us.

JUDSON. Oh, I won't. I'm going to read about you first thing tomorrow.

MAD HATTER. A-hem! *(He points to his watch.)*

JUDSON. *Today.*

ALICE. Goodbye, Judson.

DOROTHY. Goodbye. *(They kiss him simultaneously on the cheeks.)*

ALICE. And don't rub it off! *(ALL laugh. A dog barks offstage.)*

DOROTHY *(looking offstage)*. It's Toto. There he is. Come on, everybody. We have to go. Goodbye, Alice and all you wonderful Wonderland people.

ALICE. Cheerio, Dorothy. Good luck in Oz, everyone. *(ALL wave to each other and bid each other goodbye.)*

DOROTHY. Judson, hurry and put your costume together before your alarm clock goes off. *(ALL except JUD-SON exit.)*

JUDSON. Costume? Oh, yeah, the costume. Gloves, coat, tail, axe, scarf and hat. Yeah. I think I can do it. I may not win the blue ribbon, but at least I'll have a costume. But—but what character will I be?

DOROTHY'S VOICE *(offstage)*. Look, everybody. I think we've found the Yellow Brick Road that leads to the Wizard.

ALICE'S VOICE *(offstage)*. Look, there's the rabbit hole in Wonderland.

JUDSON. Wizard...Wonderland...*(Pondering it.)* The Wizard...of Wonderland. Not bad. Not bad at all. That's the character I'll be. *(An alarm clock is heard offstage.)*

MOTHER'S VOICE *(offstage)*. Judson! Wake up! Time for school now.

JUDSON *(calling offstage)*. Hey, Mom. I need to borrow some safety pins for my costume. And can you drive me to school this morning? The Wizard of Wonderland should never have to ride a bus. *(He exits.)*

## CURTAIN

## CURTAIN CALLS

*(As the curtain reopens, the SCARECROW and WHITE RABBIT enter and bow. They are followed by the DOR-MOUSE and TIN MAN, then by the LION and MAD HATTER. Next are the WITCH and QUEEN, followed by DOROTHY and ALICE. Finally, JUDSON enters dressed in his "Wizard of Wonderland" costume. Pinned to it is a blue ribbon. He points to the ribbon and ALL applaud.)*

ALL *(singing)*.

> **THANK YOU FOR COMING TODAY.**
> **MAY FANTASIES FOLLOW YOUR WAY.**
> **THE OZ AND THE WONDERLAND TEAM**
> **HOPE YOU HAD A WONDERFUL DREAM!**

## THE END

# PRODUCTION NOTES

## PROPS

| | |
|---|---|
| Pocket watch | White Rabbit |
| Axe | Tin Man |
| Oil can | Dorothy |
| Scarecrow | Judson |
| (resembling real Scarecrow) | |
| Pocket watch | Mad Hatter |
| Broom | Witch |
| Book | Witch |
| Calling cards | Mad Hatter |
| (3 used each performance) | |
| "Drink Me" bottle | Alice |
| Head Hacking Hicky | Queen |
| Book | Queen |
| Blue Ribbon | Judson |

## SOUND EFFECTS (Available on tape from the publisher)

1. Opening offstage voices of Dorothy, Alice, White Rabbit, Witch and Queen's laughter (with echo effect*).

2. Fanfare/offstage Man's voice/Drumroll (For Queen's entrance).

3. Drumroll/Fanfare (for Queen's exit).

4. Offstage voices of Witch and Queen* (Before Jabberwock entrance).

5. Alarm clock/Mother's voice.

*These voices as well as other offstage sounds may be done live if desired.

## SONGS

OPENING ............................... Judson
"STAY WITH ME" ......... Judson, Dorothy and Alice
"JABBERWOCKY" ..... All (except Witch and Queen)
"WE COULD HAVE BEEN LIKE THEM"

Witch and Queen

"PERFECT TOGETHER" ...All (except Witch and Queen)
CURTAIN CALL (TAG) ...................... All

(Incidental and underscoring selections are contained in
the full piano score).

# DIRECTOR'S NOTES

# DIRECTOR'S NOTES

# DIRECTOR'S NOTES

# DIRECTOR'S NOTES